The Antarctic Ditty Bag

A sailor's bag holding useful stuff

Tony Soper

Venture Books

First published 2021
Text copyright © Tony Soper

venturebooks@icloud.com

The author and publisher have made every effort to ensure the accuracy of the information in this book at the time of going to press. They cannot accept any responsibility for any loss, injury, or inconvenience resulting from the use of information contained herein.

All rights reserved. No part of this publication may be reproduced, stored in a retrieval system, or transmitted in any form or by any means, electronic, mechanical, photocopying, recording or otherwise without the prior consent of the publisher.

British Library Cataloguing in Publication Data
A catalogue record for this book is available from the British Library.

ISBN-13: 978-0-9553801-1-2

Design: Diane Reynolds
Front cover photo: Justin Hofman
Other photos by Tony Soper unless otherwise credited.

Thanks to Hilary Soper for critical reading of the text and to Diane Reynolds for masterly handling of the design.

Contents

Introduction	5
The Convergence	9
Discovery	11
Exploitation	17
Exploration	38
Tourism	62
Acknowledgments	113
Index	116

> How fresh was every sight and sound
> On open main or winding shore!
> We knew the merry world was round,
> And we might sail for evermore.
> —*The Voyage*, Alfred, Lord Tennyson

INTRODUCTION

As zodiac driver, wildlife lecturer and expedition leader in a string of ex-research vessels, icebreakers and other ships, I have enjoyed a dozen summer seasons exploring the Southern Ocean, coastal Antarctica and its islands.

For many years scientists had the Antarctic to themselves as a test-bed for research, and they were not at first enthusiastic about the arrival of tourists in the early 1990s. But we brought a fresh eye on the shameful mess the scientists had made of their housekeeping. Stations were often surrounded by a ring of unsightly detritus. A massive tidy-up job was one of the happy results. But the most important was that tourists went back home full of enthusiasm for Antarctic conservation.

The continental mass is a desert of ice but all around the edge there is a spectacularly mountainous coast and a splendour of islands, edged by beaches which are home to astonishing numbers of penguins and an assorted mix of blue-eyed shags, polar skuas, snowy petrels and giant stinkers. And elephant seals, four tons of steaming somnolence, gathered in companionable clumps and making the most vulgar noises you've ever encountered. Best of all, these creatures are pretty much indifferent to our arrival, treating us as harmless visitors. It's their space. This is a book remembering some of my writings and the many questions which have exercised me through the years of sailing with expedition cruise guests. A dittybag of fascinating odds and ends.

Icebreaker Kapitan Khlebnikov *lying alongside the fast ice off Coulman Island in the Ross Sea, home of a thriving colony of emperor penguins.*

The Arctic is an ocean ringed (almost) by land. The Antarctic is a continent ringed by ocean.

Cartographers draw the polar circles at latitude 66°33', with the advantage that they offer equal size of the enclosed area. But whereas the Arctic Circle encloses forests, tundra, farmland, cities like Murmansk and Tromso, industrial complexes and millions of people, including indigenous Inuit, the Antarctic Circle rings a continental snow desert without trees, shrubs or significant ground cover and only a few transient people.

Latitude for latitude, the southern hemisphere is colder than the northern. King George Island at 62°S has a mean summer temp -2°C. Anchorage, Alaska, at 61°12'N, enjoys +20°C. Greenland has an ice cap, but one-tenth the area of the Antarctic

Biologists look for ecological boundaries, dividing lines between plant and animal communities. In the Arctic the tree line forms the outer limit, beginning with the tundra and extending north to the frozen ocean and the pole. In the Antarctic the Convergence is the accepted outer limit, with a profound difference between the warm, highly productive roaring forties and the less productive frozen continent.

Both regions have plants, but the Arctic is lush by comparison. Greenland alone has over forty species, while there are only two in the Antarctic continent. Both are home to huge numbers of relatively few species of birds in their summers.

> *A paucity of species but an abundance of individuals is a recurring evolutionary motif in polar areas.*
> —David Campbell, *The Crystal Desert*

The Southern Ocean and Antarctica, David McCutcheon © Bradt Guides

THE ANTARCTIC CONVERGENCE

The Antarctic Convergence is the circumpolar region, conveniently drawn as a line undulating between 50° and 60° S, but well defined by thermometer readings – it is sometimes marked by a localised belt of fog or mist – where the warm, more saline surface currents coming south from the tropics meet the cold, denser and mainly non-saline waters moving north from the Antarctic. These conflicting currents clash, converge and sink. The mixing waters provide nutrients and a sympathetic environment for an abundance of plankton, so the Convergence nourishes huge numbers of seabirds and sea mammals.

Note that South Georgia lies south of the Convergence and thus qualifies biologically as an Antarctic Island (unlike the Falklands, for example). By contrast with the relatively barren Peninsula, in South Georgia there are 26 species of vascular plants and rather more introductions, some of which naturalised and caused problems.

The Arctic tern is the only bird to breed in the High Arctic and winter below the Convergence, spanning the globe annually.

Andreas Trepte

Jodocus Hondius, 1583

There must be a beginning of any great matter, but the continuing unto the end until it be thoroughly finished yields the true glory.
—Sir Francis Drake in a dispatch to Sir Francis Walsingham, 17 May 1587.

DISCOVERY

Who was first to reach Antarctica?

Francis Drake was a Plymouth man, sailing in search of trade and plunder on behalf of Elizabeth I. Rounding Cape Horn in 1578 his vessel *Pelican* was blown far south in a violent storm, proving in the process that Tierra del Fuego was not part of the conjectural Antarctic continent. He didn't discover land but gave his name to the notorious Drake's Passage.

> *Large numbers of icebergs are sometimes found in the area. Vessels have been lost as a consequence. The region should be navigated with great caution. Storms are frequent, visibility is often poor.* —The Antarctic Pilot

Wandering albatrosses are at home sailing the Southern Ocean in search of fish, even in foul weather.

Captain James Cook sailed south to observe a transit of Venus

In 1768, **Cook's** first voyage had the secondary object of searching the south Pacific for signs of the postulated southern continent of Terra Australis. He was first to cross the Antarctic Circle (66° 33'S) with HMS *Resolution,* on 17 January 1773, quick to take advantage of the glacier ice he encountered. As frozen fresh water the 'ice islands' have always been a godsend in watering ships (to say nothing of its value in gin and tonic).

...we bore down to an island to leeward of us; there being about it some loose ice, part of which we saw break off. There we brought-to; hoisted out three boats; and in about five or six hours, took up as much ice as yielded fifteen tons of good fresh water. The water was perfectly sweet and well-tasted.

William Hodges's drawings in Cook's Circumnavigation of Antarctica

On his second great voyage, in pursuit of the hypothetical *Terra Australis*, Cook failed to sight land but reached 71°10' S.

> The southern half of the horizon was enlightened by the reflected rays of the Ice. The clouds were of a perfect Snow whiteness and were difficult to distinguish from the ice hills. The edge of this immense Icefield was composed of loose or broken Ice so close packed together that nothing could enter it. It was indeed my opinion as well as that of most on board that this Ice extended quite to the pole or perhaps joins some land to which it had been fixed from creation.

He now swept the Southern Ocean, sailing over the predicted Terra Australis and confirming that it didn't exist. On 16 January 1775 he reached South Georgia, making the first landing, claiming sovereignty for the crown.

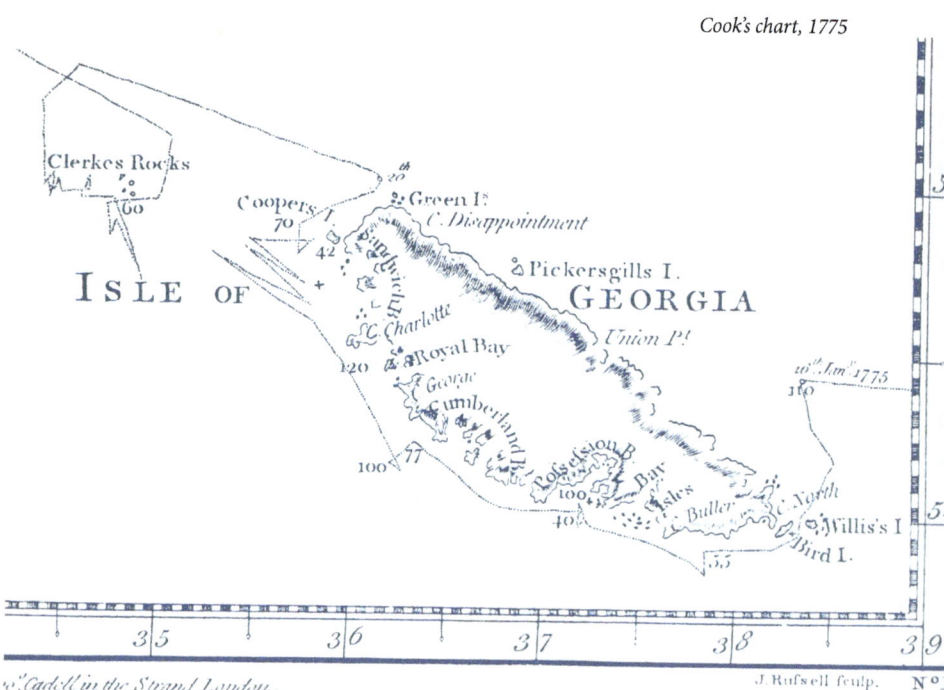

Cook's chart, 1775

I displayed our colours and took possession of the country in His Majesty's name, under a discharge of small arms.

Captain Cook displayed the British flag, and performed the ceremony of taking possession 'in the name of his Britannic Majesty, and his heirs for ever'. A volley of two or three muskets was fired into the air to give greater weight to this assertion; and the barren rocks echoed to the sound, to the utter amazement of the seals and penguins, the inhabitants of these newly-discovered dominions. —George Forster (naturalist with Cook).

Mr Forster shott an Albatross whose plumage was of a Dark grey Colour, its head, upper sides of the Wings rather inclining to black with white Eye brows. Some of the Seamen call them Quaker Birds, from their grave Colour...
—Captain James Cook, on board HMS *Resolution*, 12 January 1773

He named the island after King George III and its most abundant inhabitant king as he thought the penguin was probably the grandest and largest of its kind. But he didn't like South Georgia...

Lands doomed by Nature to perpetual frigidness, never to feel the warmth of the sun's rays, whose horrible and savage aspect I have not words to describe. Such are the lands we have discovered, what then may we expect those to be, which lie still further to the south? For we may reasonably suppose that we have seen the best, as lying most to the north. If anyone should have resolution and perseverance to clear up this point by proceeding farther than I have done, I shall not envy him the honour of the discovery.

First to sight continental Antarctic

Rounding Cape Horn, on passage in the Blythe brig *Williams* from Montevideo to Valparaiso, Capt. William Smith was forced even more to the south than Drake. Finding shelter in the lee of an island on 19 February 1819, and landing on King George Island in October, he reported the wealth of seals on reaching Valparaiso. Chartered by the navy, Edward Bransfield took command and, with Smith as pilot, returned to survey. On 30 January 1820, he now claimed the South Shetlands formally for Britain. Two days earlier he (and Smith) could have claimed first sighting of the Antarctic. But Bellingshausen got there first. As a German officer in the Imperial Russian Navy, Fabian Gottlieb Thaddeus von Bellingshausen, a prominent cartographer, commanded an expedition in the sloop *Vostok* in company with Captain Lazarev of *Mirnyi*, both required to explore the Southern Ocean and to search for land in the proximity of the South Pole. As the first since Cook, the expedition crossed the Antarctic Circle on 26 January 1820. On the 28th they reached the ice-shelf off the continental coast of what we now know as Dronning Maud Land.

Andrew Robinson

The brig Williams *in the Southern Ocean*

Admiral Bellingshausen

Summarising the evidence of logs and journals, Russians claim Bellingshausen as the discoverer of the sought-after *Terra Australis*. The dates may be disputed, but whichever of them was first to see Antarctica they certainly disproved Captain Cook's opinion that ice would block access to any land in the ice-infested Southern Ocean.

EXPLOITATION

Southern fur seal, South Georgia.

On returning to Plymouth after his circumnavigation, Captain Cook published an account of the voyage. But he underestimated the commercial value of the seals he had seen in enormous numbers and the determination of men to seek them out. News of those discoveries and the wealth of animal life in the Southern Ocean unleashed fleets of sealing expeditions by mariners who had honed their skills in Arctic waters. Trade, in the form of ruthless and indiscriminate slaughter, followed the flag. Fur seal skins and the mass of oily elephant blubber brought the sealers to the Southern Ocean to kill the creatures in devastating numbers.

British sealers reached South Georgia in 1786. Americans and rapid development soon followed. By 1791 over one hundred vessels were engaged in the industry. Vast tonnages of oil were taken from South Georgia for the London market. Fur seals escaped the worst of the carnage until 1792, when Captain Daniel Greene came in the *Nancy*, out of New Haven in Connecticut. He was the first to carry fur seal skins to Canton, in China, as a speculation. Sixteen other British and American vessels were sealing in South Georgia at the same time, but it was the Americans who monopolised the fur seal trade. The Chinese market was insatiable. In 1800, in what was probably the most profitable sealing voyage ever made to South Georgia, Captain Edmund Fanning of Stonington Connecticut, with *Betsey*, took 57,000 fur seal skins and carried them direct to China, where they were used for making felt. At five or six dollars apiece, he made a killing on the Shanghai market.

British furriers didn't pay well for the pelts. Nevertheless, *patent seal wool* from the *Sea Bear of the South Seas* was advertised as superior to imports of shawls from India *for our most fashionable Ladies: they are ornamented with gold cord, India or Grecian borders and tassels, and have a very elegant and novel effect, as well as defending the fair wearer from the cold, being warmer, softer, and equally light as the Indian shawl.* —Bell's Weekly Messenger, January 1805

Jerzy Strzelecki

Sealing captains pushed ever further south in search of fresh prey. It was the 'banana belt' which suffered most. Deception Island bore the brunt of the invasion. The American sealer Nathaniel Palmer, in *Hero,* was the first to explore, in November 1820. Palmer named it on account of its outwardly deceptive appearance as a conventional island, when a narrow entrance through 'Neptune's Bellows' revealed it rather to be the exposed rim of a large and active shield volcano, 14 x 13km, ringing a flooded caldera.

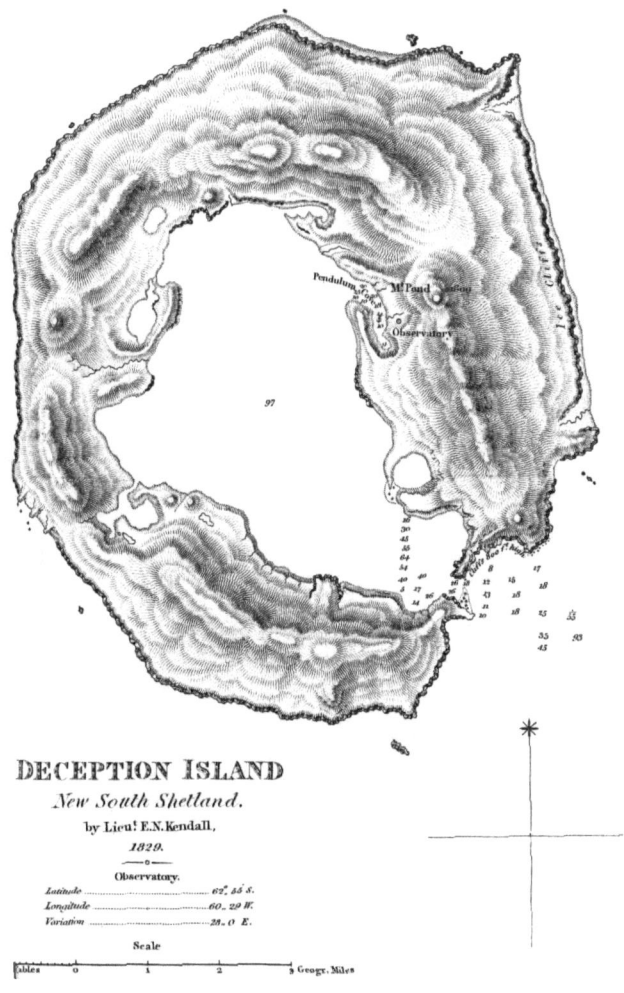

Lt. E N Kendall surveyed Neptune's Bellows, the narrow entrance to Captain Henry Foster's sheltered port in 1829.

Soon, the British and the Americans arrived to harvest the elephant seals. In 1828 Captain Henry Foster arrived with HMS *Chanticleer* to shelter in its splendid anchorage and engrave his name on the charts as Port Foster. In less than 50 years the British and Americans between them took a million and a quarter fur seals. 20,000 tons of elephant seal oil found a market in London alone (elephant seal blubber may be over 6 inches thick). In 100 years the fur seals were a remnant population, facing extermination. Commercial elephant harvesting continued till 1964, since when both populations recovered and are thriving. Today, more tourists than seals haul out on the beaches of Port Foster.

The history of sealing was a foretaste of whaling, in which a new stock was discovered and developed with good profits only to be quickly overexploited to the point of collapse, and then largely abandoned.

Killing elephant seals, Kerguelen, early nineteenth century.

...as a piece of colour the effect was gorgeous—masses of scarlet, dazzling white and blue sea. The snuffling of the seal and the sound of the blood spouting and fizzing into the snow, with the crisp sound of the steel in the quivering flesh was hardly nice; and when the red carcass sat up and looked at itself, I glanced up to see if God's eye was looking. —W G Burn Murdoch

PG Dodd

The Scot, James Weddell, came south in 1822…

…*with the Brig* Jane *and cutter* Beaufoy

On his sealing expedition, Weddell found foul weather, dense fogs and fresh gales. But on 16 January 1823, in the South Orkneys, he found a seal new to science. Taking a specimen back to the Edinburgh Royal Museum it was promptly misidentified 'Sea Leopard', inviting confusion with the leopard seal (which had already been formally described as *Phoca leptonyx* by de Blainville in 1820). Penetrating further south than any

man before, Weddell reached latitude 74° in the sea which was named in his honour. The misidentified Phoca leopardina was in fact a new species named Leptonychotes weddellii after Weddell.

Leopard seals are pagophilic – ice-loving. They even pup on an ice-floe.

Crabeater seals are gregarious and abundant. They are pretty much confined to the coast of continental Antarctica, associated with open pack (floes with many leads). They are creatures exclusively of the pack-ice, as long as there is easy access to open water. They are the most abundant seal in the world, with a population in the millions. Their scientific name is *Lobodon carcinophaga*—lobe-toothed crab eater—though they don't take crabs (which only recently arrived in the warming shallow coastal waters of Antarctica). They specialise in krill, which belong to a separate order from the decapod crabs.

Crabeaters fish for krill, timing their dives to take best advantage of the regular vertical migration patterns of Euphausia superba, the Antarctic krill. Most dives are in the top 50m but they are perfectly able to submerge for 25 minutes in a deep dive to 600m.

Ben Osborne

The **Ross seal** is a solitary animal, living in one of the remotest of all habitats, the Antarctic pack ice. A graceful and slender creature with large head and thick chest, reaching about 3m and 200 kg., slightly smaller on average than leopard and crabeater seals. Enormous eyes may be an adaptation for hunting in the dimly-lit depths. The main food source is squid and fish caught in mid-waters below the ice. The small mouth has needle-like teeth well suited to catching slippery prey.

In the breeding and moult season Ross seals haul out in areas of dense pack. Much of their life is still only dimly understood. They are very vocal, singing trills and arpeggios which carry over a great distance, so that the loneliness may be more apparent than real. Until recently it was a rare sighting, but the arrival of powerful ice-breakers and tourism means many more are being recorded. Disturbed, they raise the head and lean back in an open-jawed posture.

The French navigator **Jules-Sébastien-César Dumont d'Urville** penetrated south with *Astrolabe* and *Zélée* in search of the south magnetic pole. Reaching land on the coast of East Antarctica in January 1840, men struggled ashore, shoving aside penguins in the process, and planted the tricolour, claiming new territory for French Antarctica. *We saluted our discovery with a general hurrah. The echoes of these silent regions, for the first time disturbed by human voices, repeated our cries and then returned to their habitual silence.* d'Urville named it Terre Adélie *'in deep recognition for my devoted partner Adèle who agreed to long and painful separations'*. The penguins, though doubtless already well and truly seen by the sealers, were now formally recognised by science as *Pygoscelis adeliae*.

Men climbed down onto the ice to tie ropes to the floes...those who remained on board hauled on them to move painfully forward, while others tried to push the ice aside with picks, pincers and pickaxes... struggling to regain the open sea.

John Wildman

In 1839 the distinguished explorer **James Clark Ross** arrived in the Southern Ocean, under Admiralty instructions, in command of HMS *Erebus* and in company with HMS *Terror* (Francis Crozier). Ross heard of Dumont d'Urville's earlier successes and, 'impressed with the feeling that England had always led the way of discovery', he determined to penetrate deeper south. His were the first ships to force a way through the sea which bears his name, discovering and charting new coast in Victoria Land which he claimed for the Crown at Possession Island on 12 January 1841.

On planting the flag of our country amidst the hearty cheers of our party, we drank to the health, long life, and happiness of Her Majesty and His Royal Highness Prince Albert. Inconceivable myriads of penguins completely and densely covered the whole surface of the island, along the ledges of the precipices, and even to the summits of the hills, attacking us vigorously as we waded through their ranks, and pecking at us with their sharp beaks, disputing possession; which, together with their loud coarse notes, and the insupportable stench from the deep bed of guano, which had been forming for ages, and which may at some period be valuable to the agriculturalists of our Australasian colonies, made us glad to get away.

While it was the French who had put a name to the pesky dinner-jacketed penguins, Ross was to claim the bigger prize. In January 1842, 66° S, 156° W, *Erebus* was drifting with the pack ice, searching for a lead. On the floes were penguins new to science.

During the last few days we saw many of the great penguins, and several of them were caught and brought on board alive. These enormous birds varied in weight from sixty to seventy-five pounds. The largest was killed by the Terror's people, and weighed seventy-eight pounds. They are remarkably stupid and allow you to approach them so near as to strike them on the head with a bludgeon, and sometimes, if knocked off the ice into the water, they will almost immediately leap upon it again as if to attack you, but without the smallest means either of offence or defence. Some of these were preserved entire in casks of strong pickle, that the physiologist and comparative anatomist might have an opportunity of thoroughly examining the structure of this wonderful creature. I was in the habit of examining the stomachs of most of the birds which I shot and preserved for the Government Collection; and found the penguins my best geological collectors.

Ross waxed lyrical about the scenery...*feelings of indescribable delight upon a scene of grandeur and magnificence far beyond anything we had before seen or could have conceived.* But he saw only too clearly the impact of commercial trade. He foresaw disaster for the whales *hitherto, beyond the reach of their persecutors, they have here enjoyed a life of tranquillity and security; but will now, no doubt, be made to contribute to the wealth of our country, in exact proportion to the energy and perseverance of our merchants; and these we well know, are by no means inconsiderable. It cannot fail to be abundantly productive.* He was right, of course, seeing only too clearly the impact of commercial trade and the carnage of the whaling industry.

Commercial elephant harvesting continued till 1964.

Steam catchers and the harpoon cannon transformed the whaling industry.

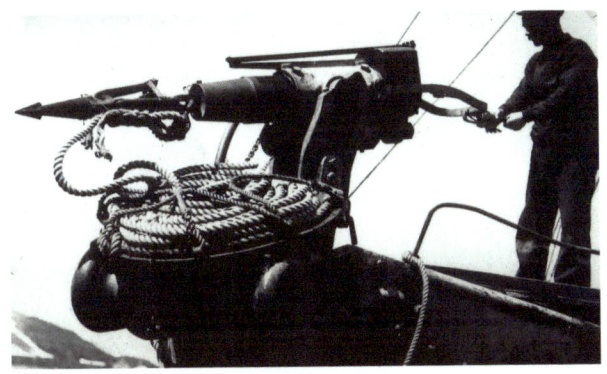

With the arrival of Svend Foyne's harpoon gun in 1870, Southern Ocean whaling flourished. Stations on South Georgia became the busiest in the world. At Grytviken, established in 1904 by Carl Larsen, more than 48,000 whales were processed, their blubber into oil for fuel, soap, margarine, their bones to meal for fertiliser and other products. But the shore-based whaling industry on South Georgia declined in response to the over-exploited population of whales around the island. Whalers abandoned South Georgia for the plentiful population further south, Deception Island became the major base for the Norwegian Hektor Company in 1911. Factory ships brought high seas pelagic whaling in the 1920s, allowing for rapid expansion. Nine factory ships in Port Foster were served by 29 catchers. In those days the 'fishery' was very wasteful, extracting only the blubber for oil and the baleen (whalebone) for corsets and umbrella makers. The massive *skrots*—skinned carcasses—were left to rot on the beaches or thrown overboard to be washed up and scavenged by petrels and skuas. In Whalers Bay, at one time, there were more than 6,000 adrift in the harbour.

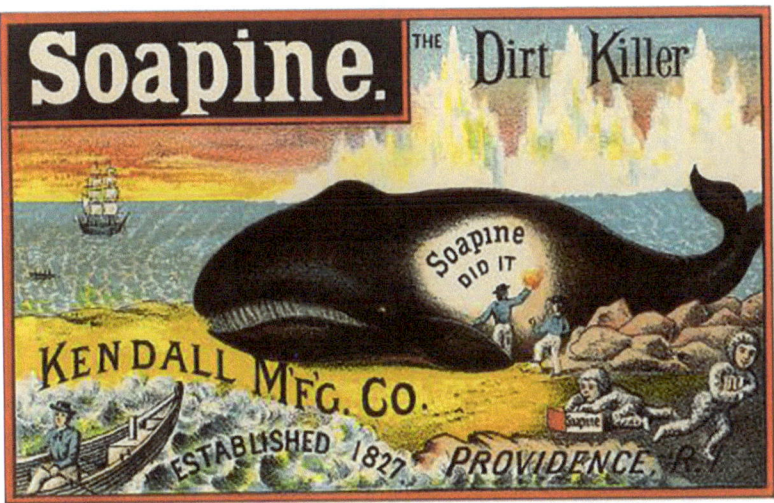

Grytviken in the 1920s

A blue whale on the plan

Christian life unfortunately does not wax strong among the whalers.
—*Clergyman, after the consecration of Capt. Larsen's church at Grytviken, 1913.*

Grytviken in the 1990s

Stinkers. Giant petrels enjoyed the greasy bounty of whaling stations.

Scavengers on every beach.

Petrels eject a foul-smelling jet of stomach oil at any unwelcome intruder which approaches too close. Whalers called giant petrels 'stinkers' from their unappetising behaviour at a carcass on the flensing plan, when they dug deep into the gaping flesh and reappeared with bloodied head and neck and aggressively widespread wings. 'Nelly' is another nickname. Nosy Nelly is American slang for a person who pokes his nose where it is not wanted; in this case into bloody carrion.

In fact, all members of the petrel family, from the mighty albatross to the sparrow-sized storm petrel, regurgitate stomach oil through mouth and nostrils. In composition it resembles the preen gland oil, and the spermaceti oil of whales. It is rich in vitamins A and D, and turns to wax when cold. It appears to be a dietary residue of the bird's oil-rich fish and crustacean diet, accumulated after the digestion of the more soluble protein component. The oil is stored in the glandular region of the stomach. It has an unpleasantly strong musky odour which clings persistently to the petrel and its nesting place, and to human flesh and clothes when an observer goes too close. The evil-smelling fluid may shoot several feet towards the visitor, since the bird is facing towards him, ready to defend itself with the hooked bill, which is opened in threat. The main function of the vomiting is in offering weight loss and easier escape flight.

The oil appears only in the stomachs of nesting petrels, and retreats later, when the chicks are bigger and are being fed more solid semi-digested marine organisms, it is in effect a store of baby-food of the right consistency. Despite its powerful smell, it is perfectly digestible.

Early whalers used the plump bodies of penguins for fuel in heating their trypots. But it represented high-quality oil and inevitably an entrepreneur arrived to exploit them in bulk. In 1891 Joseph Hatch, a New Zealander, was granted a lease to collect king and royal penguin oil at Macquarie Island. The season lasted six weeks, in which time something like 150,000 birds were processed. The birds were herded into pens before meeting their end in the 'digesters'. So long as the number taken in a season did not exceed the potential annual increase, the system could, and almost did, continue indefinitely.

The episode lasted more than 25 years, and was highly successful financially, but finally succumbed in the face of organised public opposition. A 'boiling alive' story, widely believed, had the general public and scientific societies howling for his blood. He survived a great deal of organised opposition and litigation, but the final straw for the public came when he claimed that there were more penguins on Macquarie than when he had begun operations. Hatch was branded a liar as well as a rogue. Scientists have since studied all the available data and come to the conclusion that Joseph Hatch was correct, and that in fact the population was expanding in size during the period of his depredations.

On Macquarie Island today the digesters lie idle...

...and the kings flourish

Dawn of the exploration age

Glittering white, shining blue, raven black, in the light of the sun the land looks like a fairy-tale. Pinnacle after pinnacle, peak after peak, crevassed, wild as any land on our globe, it lies, unseen and untrodden.
—Roald Amundsen, first mate of the Belgica in the Lemaire Channel.

The Belgian Antarctic Expedition, first to overwinter

In July 1895, the Sixth International Geographical Congress met in London. It encouraged exploration of the Antarctic Regions. Adrien Victor Joseph de Gerlache, of the Royal Belgian Navy, persuaded the Brussels Geographical Society to organise a successful national subscription. They named a 250 ton barque *Belgica* and appointed de Gerlache as leader. A mixed bag of scientists from various nationalities gathered. Dr. Frederick A. Cook, a 32-year-old native of Sullivan County, New York joined as surgeon, Roald Amundsen as first mate, both unpaid, looking for Antarctic experience and glory.

Sailing from Antwerp in August 1897 They reached the coast of Graham Land, then worked slowly between the coast and a long string of (the Shetland) islands to the west in what is now known as the Gerlache Strait. But they became trapped in the Bellingshausen sea ice at 70°30'S, in February 1898. The crew endured a winter 'imprisoned in an endless sea of ice' for which they were poorly prepared. Warm clothing had to be improvised, canned food lacked nutrition, penguins and seals collected and their meat stored before the onset of the dark polar night.

Scurvy became a problem. That it was caused by a deficiency of vitamin C was not to be known for another twenty years, but after his experiences in the Arctic Cook was correctly convinced that fresh meat was a cure. Cook and Amundsen took command when de Gerlache succumbed and was bunkbound.

In January 1899, *Belgica* was still trapped in ice about seven feet thick and the possibility of a second winter in the ice was becoming real. Open water was visible about half a mile away and the weakened crew used dynamite to create a channel. On 14 March they reached open water, returning to Antwerp on 5 November 1899. In spite of the circumstances, the expedition collected a significant amount of scientific data, including a full year of meteorological observations.

The British Antarctic Expedition 1898-1900 (The Southern Cross Expedition)

First to winter ashore

I was sitting foremost in the boat, and jumped ashore as the boat struck, saying, I have then the honour of being the first man who has ever put foot on South Victoria Land.

Carsten Egeburg Borchgrevink raised £40,000 from the publisher George Newnes and came to Antarctica with the ice-strengthened whaler *Southern Cross*. Sailing from London on 22 August 1898 they reached Tasmania and cleared the port of Hobart on 17 December. On board were seventy dogs and two Laplanders employed to work the sledges. Ice was found on 30 December at 61°56' but it took another 43 days to break through to see the continent on 15 February 1899. The expedition landed two days later on the flat gravel, western side of Cape Adare, and erected a prefabricated hut of Norwegian pine.

Relations with his scientists were never very cordial and their hut nearly burnt down but several short survey trips were achieved. The expedition retreated in February 1900 with one of the scientists commenting 'we are not sorry to leave this gelid, desolate spot, our place of abode for so many dreary months'. But they were the first to winter ashore in Antarctica. Borchgrevink was made a Fellow of the Royal Geographical Society.

Adelies cluster around the hut, renovated and cared for by the New Zealand Antarctic Heritage Trust

The Swedish South Polar Expedition 1901-03

Antarctic, *wintering in Cumberland Bay, South Georgia*

On a whaling recce Captain Carl Anton Larson (of South Georgia fame) found fossils on Seymour Island (off the eastern end of the Peninsula), evidence of an earlier warm climate. He returned in 1901, sailing from Göteborg, in command of *Antarctic*, for the Swedish Antarctic Expedition. Otto Nordenskjöld (son of Adolf Erik of Northeast Passage fame), led the enterprise, whose object, in those early days of heroic exploration, was a comprehensive scientific and exploration programme. After first work in the South Shetlands they reached Snow Hill Island (close to Seymour) to construct a hut for a party of six men stationed there to overwinter 1902/03. *Antarctic* retreated to winter in the Falkland Islands and South Georgia before planning to return in the summer of 03 to relieve the Snow Hill station. Ice prevented the ship from reaching the island so a three-man sledge party was landed at Hope Bay in the Antarctic Sound and dispatched over the ice to collect and bring the six men there to await the ship. *Antarctic* then went back for another attempt to pass the ice fields.

The sledge party, led by Johan Andersson, crossed to the east side of the Peninsula but found impassable open water and had to return to Hope Bay to wait the return of *Antarctic*. The ship, however, was beset in pack-ice

The historic Andersson shelter at Hope Bay.

south of Paulet Island, and eventually crushed and sank. Her complement of twenty men landed on the island after a difficult lifeboat-haul across the ice. They had sufficient equipment and supplies, supplemented with penguin meat and eggs, to endure tolerable circumstances, but their position was unknown to anyone. Only they knew the full implications of the expedition's plight. They built themselves a stone-walled hut, roofed with spars and canvas and stored many penguins and seals.

The Larson hut today.

Three separate groups from the expedition now faced winter. The Antarctic crew in their hut on Paulet. The six Snow Hill Island men at their base with no news about what happened to the expected ship and no certainty that anyone knew of their situation. The three Hope Bay men awaited return of the ship, though as time passed it became apparent that they were marooned. All parties faced a very severe winter.

In the 1903-04 spring the Hope Bay three set off again, this time finding firm pack-ice to Snow Hill Island. On the way they met two men from that station at Cape Wellmet, before they reunited with the rest of the Snow Hill group. At much the same time Captain Larsen, with a small party aboard one of the lifeboats saved from *Antarctic*, reached Hope Bay where he found a message revealing that the men had left for Snow Hill Island.

Meanwhile three search expeditions had sailed: the Argentine Navy's corvette *Uruguay* (Capt. Julian Irizar), *Français* (Capt. Jean-Baptiste Charcot), and the Swedish *Frithiof* (Capt. Hans Gylden). On 8 November 1903 *Uruguay* reached Snow Hill Island. Late that evening the sledge dogs started barking, Captain Larsen with the lifeboat party had arrived. All three parties of the lost expedition were united on this 'Day of Wonders'. After stopping at Paulet Island to relieve those from *Antarctic* who had remained there, *Uruguay* returned in triumph to Buenos Aires. The expedition returned to Göteborg in December 1903. Despite the great hardships endured it was considered a scientific success, having explored much of the eastern coast of Graham Land and the Palmer Archipelago and recovered valuable geological and fossil samples. Nordenskjöld enjoyed fame at home, but its huge cost left him greatly in debt.

Today the station on Snow Hill Island, the refuge at Hope Bay, and the hut on Paulet Island are historical monuments proclaimed under the provisions of the Antarctic Treaty. *Uruguay* is berthed as a museum ship in Buenos Aires, one of the historic ships of the port. The men of the expedition always celebrated 8 November and their descendants continue the practice. For the Antarctic community in general, and especially in Scandinavia, it is a very significant date in Antarctic exploration.

The Snow Hill hut today

Tim Soper

The rescue vessel Uruguay *in honourable retirement, Buenos Aires*

Roberto Fiadone

The Discovery Expedition 1901

For sheer downright misery give me a hurricane, not too warm, the yard of a sailing ship, a wet sail and a bout of sea sickness
—Apsley Cherry-Garrard, *The Worst Journey in the World*

Captain Robert Falcon Scott, RN., led two expeditions to the Antarctic: the Discovery Expedition 1901–1904 and the ill-fated Terra Nova Expedition 1910–1913. On the first, he set a new southern record by sledging to 82° S and discovering the Antarctic Plateau. On the second, he led a party of five which reached the South Pole on 17 January 1912, five weeks after Roald Amundsen. A planned rendezvous with supporting dog teams from the base camp failed, 150 miles from their base camp and 11 miles from the next depot. Scott and his companions perished.

RRS Discovery

Scott was devoted to scientific research, and on the return leg his party collected plant fossils, proving Antarctica was once forested, part of the supercontinent Pangaea before it broke away in the early Mesozoic.

The Scott hut at Discovery Point, McMurdo

Scott, the fossil collector

Herbert Ponting

Glaciers are the source of the mighty ice shelves which ring the Antarctic continent. The Ross ice shelf formed 'The Great Ice Barrier' of the Scott expedition.

Aurora Australis, the Southern Lights

Ghostly flickerings and patterns of light, draperies of reds to violets and greens, subtly fill the winter sky, rising and falling in intensity. Best seen around the Ross Sea area and the coast of east Antarctica, and among the most beautiful of natural phenomena, the Southern Lights are not fully understood. They may be due to electrically charged streams of particles shot from the flaming surface of the sun. Pulled towards the magnetic poles, they produce displays of light dozens of miles in the sky when they collide with the atmosphere.

An aurora is classified as either diffuse or discrete. A diffuse aurora is a featureless glow in the sky that may not be visible to the naked eye even on a dark night and defines the extent of the auroral zone. Discrete auroras are sharply-defined features; they vary in brightness from barely visible to bright enough for reading a newspaper at night.

From Scott base, McMurdo

Swaying auroral light ... fold on fold the arches and curtains of vibrating luminosity rise and spread across the sky, to slowly fade and yet again spring to glowing life.' —Robert Falcon Scott, *Journal*

The British 1907-1909 Nimrod Expedition

Some of us are over the seasick stage and we no longer want to die.
—Second officer Arthur Harbord after ten days aboard *Nimrod* with Shackleton.

The barquentine ex-sealer Nimrod

The forces of these uncontrollable icepacks are stronger than human resolution. —Shackleton

Difficulties are just things to be overcome. —Shackleton

Frank Hurley

The Nimrod Expedition was an early attempt in the race to the geographic South Pole led by the young Ernest Shackleton. His base was established at Cape Royds. The hut had separate stabling for the expedition's ponies, dog kennels and the first motorcar on the continent, a 12-15 horsepower Arrol Johnston. The party lived here through the winter of 1908, before the attempt at the pole. Shackleton left it in good order, stocked with provisions and equipment to last fifteen men for a year. The hut was locked and the key nailed on the door. Today the Antarctic Heritage Trust has custody over the Historic Site, and by 2008 the structure was fully restored to the condition when Shackleton's team left it.

Amongst other things, several crates of Mackinlay's Rare Old Highland Malt whisky were found buried under the hut. In 2009 a team from the New Zealand Antarctic Trust defrosted a single crate. Still wrapped in their protective paper and straw, ten bottles survived, the precious liquid inside perfectly intact. Three were flown, by private jet, to Scotland, where a Mackinlay team found the whisky's strength to be 47.3%, that it contained peat from the Orkney Islands, and that it had been aged in American white oak sherry casks.

The Australasian Antarctic Expedition

Douglas Mawson, Alistair McKay and Edgworth David at the south magnetic pole, January, 1909

Australian Antarctic Division

Having taken part in Shackleton's 1907-09 Nimrod expedition, Douglas Mawson, an Australian geologist, came up with a plan to explore that part of Antarctica directly below Australia, charting the 2,000 mile-long coastline of Antarctica to the south of Australia. between 1911 and 1914. Unlike both of Shackleton's expeditions, which produced very little science, advances were made in geology, glaciology and terrestrial biology. Mawson was knighted for his achievements as a leader.

The location chosen for the main base camp, at Cape Denison, proved to be one of the places on Earth with the strongest wind forces. In polar regions, the strongest winds are born in the cold air of the ice-cap, blowing down steep slopes and accelerating under gravity. These 'katabatic' - down-flowing - winds reach fearsome speeds, with 120mph common. In the Mawson expedition, the Australians recorded gusts of up to 140mph were recorded, breaking the anemometer. Katabatics die as abruptly as they arrive, to be followed by other trials. A gale of wind following a snowfall lifts the new snow and creates blizzards, when the driven snow has the erosive power of sand, penetrating everywhere, polishing rocks and making travel difficult or even impossible.

Conditions are wild even a few metres from the shore in a katabatic.

The Imperial Trans-Antarctic Expedition 1914–17

For a joint scientific and geographical piece of organisation, give me Scott; for a Winter Journey, Wilson; for a dash to the Pole and nothing else, Amundsen; and if I am in the devil of a hole and want to get out of it, give me Shackleton every time.
—Apsley Cherry-Garrard

Conceived by Ernest Shackleton, this was the last major expedition of the heroic age of Antarctic Exploration, an attempt to make the first land crossing of the Antarctic continent. Failing to accomplish this objective, the expedition became recognised instead as an epic feat of survival.

Frank Hurley

Within a few seconds she heeled over until she had a list of thirty degrees to port.

Endurance became beset in the ice of the Weddell Sea and drifted, held in the pack ice, throughout the Antarctic winter of 1915. Eventually crushed and sunk, she stranded 28 men on the ice. After months of northwards drift, the party took to the lifeboats to reach the inhospitable, uninhabited Elephant Island.

Point Wild, the inhospitable base on Elephant Island.

Frank Wild was in charge of crew morale. Reginald James composed a verse to celebrate his prowess.

> *My name is Franky Wild-o and my hut's on Elephant Isle.*
> *The wall's without a single brick and the roof's without a tile.*
> *Yet, nevertheless, you must confess by many and many a mile,*
> *It's the most palatial dwelling place you'll find on Elephant Isle.*

Leaving most of his crew in the relative safety of their upturned boat at Cape Wild, Shackleton set off with five companions in the open whaler *James Caird* to face 800 miles of wild ocean in one of the greatest small boat voyages of all time, towards South Georgia. Achieving landfall, and without a map, they improvised a route from Peggoty Bluff across mountain and glaciers to the whaling station at Stromness. It was the first confirmed crossing of the South Georgia interior.

The foam of the breaking sea surged white around us. We felt our boat lifted and flying forward like a cork in a breaking surf.
—Ernest Shackleton

Everybody knew Shackleton well, and we very sorry he lost in ice with all hands. We not know three terrible-looking bearded men who walk into office off the mountainside. Manager say: 'Who the hell are you?' and terrible bearded man in centre of the three men say very quietly: 'My name is Shackleton'. Me I turn aside and weep. I think Manager weep too.
—Mansell, Norwegian office worker in the Manager's office.

The managers office was at the extreme left of the whaling station at Stromness.

The southern winter and ship problems inevitably meant delay and it was three months before Shackleton sailed with the steam-tug *Yelcho*, commanded by Luis Pardo, for the relief and rescue of the men at Elephant. Without the loss of a man, the entire party was brought to Punta Arenas in Chile on 3 September 1916.

Yelcho arriving at Valparaiso.

The Shackleton-Rowett Expedition of 1921-22

Shackleton's last Antarctic project is better known by the name of his vessel *Quest*. Smaller than any recent Antarctic exploration ship, she soon proved inadequate for the task, and progress south was delayed. Before the expedition's work could properly begin, Shackleton died on board the ship, just after arriving at South Georgia. It may be seen as the final episode in the Heroic Age of Antarctic Exploration.

Six years later when looking at Shackleton's grave and the cairn which we, his comrades, erected to his memory on a windswept hill of South Georgia, I meditated on his great deeds. It seemed to me that among all his achievements and triumphs, great as they were, his one failure was the most glorious. By self-sacrifice and throwing his own life into the balance he saved every one of his men - not a life was lost - although at times it had looked unlikely that one could be saved. His outstanding characteristics were his care of, and anxiety for, the lives and well-being of all his men.
—Frank Worsley

I hold that a man should strive to his uttermost for his life's set prize.
—Robert Browning, on Shackleton's headstone

The British Graham Land expedition 1934-37

Britain formally claimed the island of Deception in 1908 and its scientific station 'B' became the administrative centre for all whaling activities in the South Shetlands. At this time Graham Land (named after Sir James Graham, First Lord of the Admiralty at the time of John Biscoe's exploration in 1832) was generally supposed to be an archipelago. Based at Deception and commanded by John Riddoch Rymill, the geophysical and exploration expedition used a combination of traditional and modern practices; dog teams and motor sledges as well as aircraft. They spent a successful two years in the Antarctic, as part of which they certainly determined that British Graham Land was part of a peninsula.

The aircraft—a De Havilland Fox Moth (G-ACRU) capable of operating with skis or floats—was used extensively for reconnaissance, aerial surveying and depot laying. Plane trips were limited by the safe range of the aircraft which was some 280 miles or three and a half hours flying time. Often weather conditions precluded flights for many days and other limitations included low cloud and unsuitable landing surfaces. However, the aircraft proved invaluable for route finding, surveying and depot laying and was used with skis or floats as conditions allowed.

Fox Moth G-ACRU on skis aerial surveying and depot laying.

SPRI

Deception and Operation Tabarin

By 1938, Deception had a post office, a stipendiary magistrate, and telegraph communications. At the height of the Second World War, in 1943, the British Government launched a top-secret expedition involving a base on the island. The role of Operation Tabarin was ostensibly to collect meteorological information and deny safe anchorages to enemy raiding vessels, but from the outset survey and science was planned. From 1944, this work was carried out by the Falkland Islands Dependencies Survey (forerunner of the British Antarctic Survey). Tabarin also actively reinforced British territorial claims at a time when this was being challenged.

In the 1950's aerial surveys were served by the aeroplane hangar which survives today. The British Antarctic Survey's de Havilland Otter VPFAK flew in support of field teams and dog parties. Damaged by a gale in October 1961 and by a crevasse accident at Adelaide Island 19 December 1964 it was grounded at Deception due to extensive metal fatigue in 1967. We saw the sad fuselage in its last years till 2004 when it was taken first to Rothera and then repatriated to the UK for restoration. Currently it is held by the de Havilland Aircraft Museum at London Colney.

The station was evacuated on 5 Dec 1967 after volcanic eruptions, then again on 21 Feb 1969 when further eruptions damaged buildings at Pendulum Cove and Whaler's Bay. On both occasions personnel were evacuated by the Chilean research vessel *Piloto Pardo*. The base was finally abandoned on 23 Feb 1969, to be rediscovered by tourism in the nineties.

Biscoe House

The geothermally heated waters of Whalers Bay make way for the famous polar plunge

The Tourist Age

As a tourist destination, continental Antarctica involves 600 miles of what can be an uncomfortable crossing of the Drake: several days with a ship enjoying what can often be described as a lively motion. An uninterrupted wind circulates vigorously to develop into the notorious 'roaring forties, furious fifties and screaming sixties'—the West Wind Drift.

The research vessel Professor Molchanov sails from Ushuaia for a tourist trip to continental Antarctica…

…finding sooty shearwaters along the coast.

J J Harrison

Cape Horn is a rocky headland in the Tierra del Fuego archipelago. It marks the southern tip of South America and overlooks the strait where the Pacific and Atlantic oceans meet. The cape lies within Chilean territory and the Chilean Navy maintains a station on Hornos Island.

A short distance from it is a memorial sculpture made by José Balcells featuring the silhouette of an albatross, commemorating the lives of the many seafarers who perished attempting to sail around the Horn.

I am the albatross that waits for you
at the end of the earth.
I am the forgotten soul of the dead sailors
who crossed Cape Horn
from all the seas of the world.
   —Peter Oxford's translation of Sara Vial's poem, *Soy el albatros*

The Drake Passage

Large numbers of icebergs are sometimes found in the area. Vessels have been lost as a consequence. The region should be navigated with great caution. Storms are frequent, visibility is often poor. —The Antarctic Pilot

The highest frequency of gales is reported between longitudes 20° and 60°E, north of the Ross and Weddell Seas and the approaches to the Drake Passage. Interaction between the frigid air coming off Antarctica and the relatively warm and moist air from the lower latitude ocean areas, creates the cyclonic 'Roaring Forties' storms. They make the region from latitudes 40° to 60°S one of the stormiest areas in the world. The main course of these cyclones is from east to west around the periphery of Antarctica.

Southern Ocean winds blow strongly. In the furious fifties and screaming sixties there is little in their way, whipping up the West Wind Drift, the strongest sustained westerly storms found anywhere on earth. (Closer to the continent and south of 55°, contrary currents create the 'east wind drift'.)

Allan White

Black-browed albatross

Circumpolar, widely distributed and common, the **black-browed albatross** is sometimes found many hundreds of miles from land, yet it is more common in inshore waters than other albatrosses, even penetrating fjords and harbours, especially in foul weather. Commonly seen in the Beagle Channel and a welcome ship-follower for the best part of the Drake crossing, Its search pattern is typical of all albatrosses. It takes its krill and fish prey mainly by surface-seizing, but also by active plunging and diving at the surface.

Post-breeding dispersal is generally to the north, they commonly reach to 10°S off Peru and 20°S off South Africa, working the cold-water Humboldt and Benguela currents. This northward tendency may account for the regular appearance of this albatross in the Northern Hemisphere, though it is highly likely that some of them, having been caught on lines by fishermen, are 'helped' through the doldrums and released when they are no longer a novelty. Traditionally fishermen have used them as bait or cosseted them as temporary pets. They are the most abundant and widespread of all albatrosses, with a total world population of over a million, but at longterm risk. Every year fishing vessels, many of them 'pirates', unwittingly drown tens of thousands of albatrosses when the birds seize baited hooks intended for fish. This caused a catastrophic decline, threatening the existence of some species.

Cape petrels are better known to expedition staff and all Spanish-speakers as *pintados* (painted petrels). They fly in fulmar fashion, a sequence of stiff flaps followed by gliding. In gregarious flocks, they are enthusiastic ship-followers. Squid, krill and fish are the main food, taken by day and night from the surface by pecking in a pigeon-like manner (hence the seaman's name cape pigeon) but sometimes by dipping in flight. Cape petrels commonly attend trawlers for offal, take galley waste from other ships and associate with whales for scraps.

Allan White

Allan White

Not to be confused with the Antarctic petrel *Thalassoica antarctica*, which displays less of the Jackson Pollock effect, having a white trailing edge to its upperwing. Less keen on ship-following, it is often seen in peninsula waters November December, on its way to the nunataks of continental mountain ranges of the Ross and Weddell seas.

Snowy Sheathbills are strong, but markedly reluctant, flyers. In the austral spring they make long migratory flights, crossing the Drake Passage to take advantage of the thriving colonies of penguins. Not averse to assisted passage on ships, they have enjoyed galley scraps, in one case crossing the entire length of the Atlantic to a wharfside landfall at Plymouth in the British Isles.

Brown skuas are also not averse to migrating to the peninsula the easy way.

Prions, known to the early seamen as whalebirds because of the spectacular flocks which gathered to feed on the plankton disturbed by whale activity, are confined to the Southern Ocean. Small and blue-grey, they carry striking M-marks on their upper wings and have a black-tipped tail. Rather in the manner of the baleen whales they attend, they gulp water rich in copepods, and then force it out through a comb-like sieve (palatal lamellae) that acts as a filter along the side of the bill. The main food is krill, small fish and carrion taken on the wing in tern-style, but they will also forage for larger plankton animals from the edges of older pack-ice.

Fairy prions Pachyptila turtur *are birds of the open ocean, though they will shelter in the lee of a vessel in foul weather*

All seabirds have a particular problem when it comes to dealing with the quantity of salt which they inevitably ingest in both drinking and fishing. They absorb far more than their renal system can deal with. The surplus is conveyed by a network of blood vessels into fine tubes connected with the nasal glands. This concentrated sodium chloride is in solution and drips constantly from the tip of the beak.

Antarctic prion P. desolata

Circumpolar, widespread and abundant, **Wilson's storm petrel**, *Oceanites oceanicus*, is one of the most abundant bird species, with a world population estimated to be more than thirty million. Yet most people will never see one. Tiny birds, they are perfectly at home thousands of miles from land.

In feeding, foraging around the pack-ice, the bird skips, walks and patters over the surface. Fluttering and dancing, (in Peru they are known as bailarines—ballet dancers). Sometimes walking over the surface, dipping and diving for trifles of tiny fish and crustaceans, sometimes stopping for a moment with wings raised high and legs dangling, they sometimes actually go backwards. Downwind of whale-blows they scoop grease or oily matter from the condensed breath, and in company with a decomposing whale they take oil droplets as they rise to the surface.

Opportunistic feeders, they are enthusiastic ship-followers, crowding around galley waste. Krill is an important item of diet and they are indefatigable in search of concentrations. They are probably capable of smelling the way to carrion and its food potential.

'Petrel' is from the Christian name Peter, derived from the habit of 'walking on water' in biblical style, behaviour which also led to the popular name Jesus-bird. Collectively the little birds of the genus Oceanites are 'Mother Carey's Chickens', gathering in a flock commanded by that legendary, benevolent, yet sinister female deity of the sea—sinister because these little birds are said to gather around a ship in distress, ready to carry off a drowned sailor for reincarnation. A more prosaic reason for the behaviour in foul weather might be that the birds are benefitting from shelter hugging the lee side of a vessel.

Circumpolar, widespread and abundant, with a total population of many millions, this is the most commonly recorded storm-petrel in Antarctic waters and possibly the most numerous seabird in the world.

Wilson's storm-petrels are named for Alexander Wilson, the distinguished Scottish/American ornithologist author of the early 19th century American Ornithology (not for the equally-distinguished Edward Wilson, artist/doctor of Scott's expeditions).

Lying alongside the fast ice off Halley station in the Weddell Sea, a pair of Wilson's explored the possibility of nesting places in the icebreaker Kapitan Khlebnikov, showing their strikingly coloured feet.

Tim Soper

On approach to the peninsula in the occasional calm sea there may be a concentration of dozens of fin whales.

Tim Soper

John Sparks

Snow petrels are found only in association with the pack-ice and always south of 55° latitude. Sedentary birds, they never stray far from their home base. They breed in loose colonies, in crevices and hollows on mountain peaks and on nunataks. Returning to the nest sites in November, they may dig through a metre of snow to find a ground base for the nest. Eggs and chicks may be taken by skuas, but extremes of weather are a more serious cause of mortality.

Matthieu Weber

Tabular icebergs calving from the shelf-ice

Tabular icebergs are monitored worldwide by the U.S. National Ice Center, which tracks them. It assigns any larger than 10 nautical miles (19 km) along at least one axis a name composed of a letter indicating its point of origin and a running number.

A – longitude 0° to 90° W (Bellingshausen Sea, Weddell Sea)
B – longitude 90° W to 180° (Amundsen Sea, Eastern Ross Sea)
C – longitude 90° E to 180° (Western Ross Sea, Wilkes Land)
D – longitude 0° to 90° E (Amery Ice Shelf, Eastern Weddell Sea)

As sea freezes, it first forms pancake ice.

Sea ice is salty and buoyant. As floes, in a range of sizes, ages and thicknesses, it is carried along by winds and sea currents, tending to be driven together into a mass when it becomes pack ice. This may cause real problems both for shipping and for penguin colonies when it covers the surface of the sea.

Close pack. The sort of conditions offering leads open to navigation.

Icebreaker Kapitan Khlebnikov breaking multi-year ice.

Ten-tenths multi-year pack, serious trouble for any vessel.

The Emperor Penguin

Emperors breed on fast ice, in the coldest conditions endured by any bird, never touching land in their whole lives. The male takes responsibility for the single egg for the entire nine weeks of incubation in the dark Antarctic winter, carrying the egg cradled on his feet, covered by a fold of abdominal skin, and protected from the weather by huddling with the multitude of other males. The female spends the incubation period fattening at sea, returning with a full crop at about the time of the chick's emergence. Astonishingly, the male gives the naked chick's first feed, a secretion of fat and protein from its crop, before trudging off to the sea to fish, a journey which may take several days. The chick soon moults into its first 'Biggles' suit of down. Fed alternately by both parents, it joins a crèche at about six weeks of age, fledging in the spring at about five months, when the shortest walk to the maximum food is available. In a hard season, when the sea-ice persists, many chicks die of starvation. But all being well, the newly fledged or nearly fledged juveniles are carried out to sea as the ice breaks into floes. Fully independent, the young must moult to their diving plumage before their ice floe disintegrates, introducing them to the sea to dive for their own fish.

John Sparks

The most northerly colony of emperors was first seen from the air by BAS scientists, several years before we were privileged to be the first to land and see them up close. It was on 9 November 2004 that *Kapitan Khlebnikov* took a chance on spending a spare day to steam south off the exposed ocean side of Snow Hill Island. Docked into the fast ice we found adult emperors. In the afternoon on a scout flight we discovered the colony twenty miles away. It was abundantly clear that at last it was going to be a practical possibility to organise trips sailing from Ushuaia in the conventional time frame for tourists to have the unique chance of seeing the greatest of all penguins. And so it has proved.

Toboganning towards the sea edge...

...and a waiting leopard seal.

Debbie Harrison

Snowy sheathbills summer in the Antarctic peninsula. They strut about pecking for titbits in the manner of a farmyard fowl. Scavengers and kleptoparasites, they get much of their food by stealing what has already been collected by penguins and shags. Foraging amongst concentrations of penguins and shags, they take eggs and small chicks; often they stand by at feeding sessions, when they grab bits of food which have been dropped during the regurgitation process. Penguins feed their young with part-digested krill 'balls' and the sheathbills excel in intercepting them. They take readily, too, to food offered at expedition bases and campsites.

Gordon Leggett

> Who would believe in penguins, unless he had seen them?
> —Conor Cruise O Brien

> They have nothing of the taste of Flesh, and for my part, I take them to be feather'd Fish. —Pierre Sonnerat 1782

Bartolomeo Diaz was probably the first European to see the southern penguins. He reached the Cape of Good Hope in 1488 but sadly doesn't mention specific birds in his log. In 1497 he wrote of birds which brayed like asses, as big as ducks, but cannot fly.

Early explorers thought penguins were fish and classified them accordingly. In fact, as birds, they are superbly designed for their job. Their compact, streamlined bodies have a deep keel for a breastbone and massive paddle muscles. Their feathers are reduced in size and stiffened, with a fluffy aftershaft at the base. This down joins to create an insulating layer of air over a thick layer of blubber (a third of their body weight) and skin. Effectively their bodies are packed in blubber, with a string vest and a windproof outer parka. Their wings are reduced to paddles, the bones flattened, the wrist and elbow joints fused, so that although the wings can't be folded, they act as a powerful propulsion unit. The legs are set well back on the body so that the feet act as control surfaces in the water. Their heads retract to create a perfect hydrodynamic shape. In the water, they travel fast by 'porpoising' at the surface or diving in pursuit of squids, shrimps or fish. It is not easy to catch fish underwater, but penguins are well adapted. They swim with great skill. Their plumage is compressed, bones more solid than those of birds which fly. The rib cage is strong to withstand pressure in diving. In fact they fly underwater. Ashore they walk upright with a seaman's rolling gait. Some walk, some progress by jumps, some by tobogganing over ice and snow. Some can climb steep cliff faces, some leap like salmon in order to land on ice floes. They are highly sociable birds, both at sea and ashore, breeding in colonies which can involve tens of thousands of pairs.

How did penguins get their name?

When Ferdinand Magellan sailed the Atlantic coast of South America in 1520 searching a route to the spice islands of the Indies he found countless numbers of plump birds similar in shape and behaviour to the auks of the northern islands his crew knew so well. Inevitably they called them by their Portuguese name pingüim. Seamen visiting the Patagonian beaches commonly described the birds they found there 'big as geese'.

From its earliest iteration as penguin the English name evolved first, when British whalers returned from the north, to garfowl (from the Norse *geirfugl* meaning spearbird), only to be superceded logically by great auk, largest of the auk family. Linnaeus named the species *Alca impennis* – plump and flightless. (Ornithological fashion now calls it *Pinguinus impennis*).

In 1655 the giant razorbill was named penguin *by the Danish naturalist Ole Worm, from his captive Faroese specimen*

In 1605 botanist Carolus Clusius's drawing of Magellan's plump birds 'big as geese' is clearly a great auk.

The derivation is controversial. My money supports the claim of the Latin pinguis, fat. It originally served in the northern hemisphere as the name of that largest razorbill, which flourished on offshore islands of the North Atlantic. It was not only plump and upright in posture, it was flightless and it was commonly known to Basque and Portuguese fishermen well before the sixteenth century in various versions of pinguis. In French they were known as grand pinguin, in Spanish pinguino, in Portuguese pingüim and in English penguin.

In fact razorbills and its auk family are not related to the southern penguins. The similarity between them is a classic example of convergent evolution, in which animals which have the same mode of life tend to look like each other.

Fishermen worked the Newfoundland Banks for cod from the early 16th century. For bait, for feathers and for a meat dinner, they raided the nests of the plump seabirds which flourished on the offshore islands.

God made the innocence of so poor a creature to become an admirable instrument for the sustenation of man. —Richard Whitbourne 1620

The great auk's easy capture was its undoing. Taken in unsustainable numbers, first for food, then by collectors, numbers fell to the point at which they became valuable as museum specimens, the rocketing value of their eggs brought them to extinction in 1844.

Audubon painted great auks at Funk Island in the Grand Banks, in 1827, not long before the extinction which was accelerated by Collectors.

The Gentoo Penguin

Rob McCallum

Early Portuguese colonisers in India gave their name gentio (gentile/heathen) to natives from the non-Muslim community, a sect known by a white cap, later to become Hindu. It was Magellan's sailors who had brought the word *pingüim* to South America and it seems likely they also named the white-bonneted penguins (gentio corrupting to gentoo in English).

Their nest space is hotly defended. Two eggs are the normal clutch, but usually only one chick survives to fledge. Unlike most other penguins, northern gentoos will replace a lost clutch. Parents share an incubation period of 31–39 days, the chicks are fed on undigested shrimps or small fish by regurgitation. They gather in the protection of crèches at four to five weeks (allowing both adults to go fishing).

Uniquely among penguins, the young continue to be fed by their parents for a further period after fledging, so that they are hanging around the moulting area together well into March. The total population of gentoos is somewhere around 300,000 pairs.

The only surviving base from the Tabarin days, Port Lockroy, on Goudier Island, is operated by the UK Antarctic Heritage Trust. It hosts the UK's most southerly public Post Office. Around 70,000 cards are posted each year to over 100 countries. The thriving population of gentoos is unbothered by the visiting tourists.

The Macaroni Penguin

Ben Osborne

How did the macaroni get its name?

The height of eighteenth century fashion

The macaroni's name comes from the 18th century dandies who made the Grand Tour to Italy and affected ludicrous continental tastes and fashions, dyeing their hair in streaks and extending crests over their ears. Arriving back in England they were called 'macaronis' by mockers, whose only association with Italy was the pasta with which they were familiar. On exploring south, both British and US sealers, meeting the gaudily crested penguins for the first time, christened them after the hairstyle.

**Yankee Doodle went to town
Riding on a pony
Stuck a feather in his hat
And called it macaroni**

The song comes from the time of the American Revolutionary War. Richard Shuckburgh was a British army doctor serving in New York and the author of the song's lyrics. Whether or not they were being mocked by the British, the Yankees sang them with enthusiasm and the song lives on.

Macaronis thrive still today in the Southern Ocean, in music and in the Blondie cartoon, where Dagwood sports a classic macaroni.

The Spirit of 76. Archibald MacNeal Willard's celebration of the pre-revolutionary war song 'Yankee doodle'.

The Chinstrap Penguin

Chinstraps like to nest well above sea level, but in spring the coastal slopes are covered in snow. They wait patiently for bare rock to reveal itself as suitable for nest-making, and inevitably the first slopes to uncover are on the hilltops. So, in early summer, a continuous stream of penguins trudges up and down the steep slope. As the snow retreats the birds colonise more extensively and the seabird city comes to life. On the slopes of Baily Head something over a hundred thousand pairs breed in raucous community.

The icebreaker Kapitan Khlebikov at anchor off Baily Head

The highest points are first to be patronised

Both parents share incubation, closely guarding the precious small stones of nest material.

Male chinstraps are pugnacious creatures, perfectly capable of bullying an Adèlie off its nest in a takeover. In their incubation period they regularly shed the linings of their stomachs, throwing up a yellowy-orange membrane, a 'burst balloon', in pursuit of an unclear function, possibly serving to reduce parasite infestation. But why is this activity,

Stomach lining

well observed in many other bird families, seemingly confined in penguins to chinstraps?

The chicks are fattened on regurgitated krill and join a crèche after their first month or so. Fledged in 52-60 days, they go to sea while the adults begin their moult. It may be well into April and even May before the last stragglers go to sea.

As the second most abundant species of penguin it has an extremely wide range. The current increase in population is reaching towards four million pairs.

Chinstrap chicks are fattened on krill soup

Strict hygiene prevails.

Penguins in the northern hemisphere

Penguins cannot tolerate warm sea water. The extreme limit of their range is marked by a line linking places with a mean annual air temperature of 20° C (surface waters are warmed accordingly), so they are effectively trapped by a thermal barrier and restricted to the cold waters of the southern hemisphere, though nitpickers will point out that a small population of Galapagos penguins just straddles across into the north. By the same token polar bears, caribou and muskox are unable to cross to the south, where polar bears would probably do well in a seal-rich Antarctic environment.

An ill-fated experiment introduced a small number of king, macaroni and jackass penguins to Røst in the Lofoten Islands, off the Norwegian coast, in the late 1930's. The last recorded sighting of a survivor was in 1954. Some suffered at the hands of local people who regarded them as bogeymen. None attempted to nest, probably because there weren't enough of them to encourage the noisy sociability which stimulates courtship. They do well in zoos when they are in close company.

Noel Kirkpatrick

Skuas

The name 'skua' comes from the Icelandic *skufr* and is doubtless a rendering of their chase-calls in flight. Long and dark, skuas look superficially like immature gulls, but they are heavier, more robust and menacing in mien, as befits birds of prey. They have conspicuous white patches at the base of the primaries. Theirs is a piratical nature and they have hawk-like beaks to serve it. As kleptoparasites, they are opportunistic feeders, but fish and krill are a major part of their prey.

Half a dozen species in two genera breed in the high latitudes of both hemispheres. Much learned discussion revolves around the question of how many species are present in the deep south, since distinct populations exist on various island groups. In Antarctica, the main contenders are the south polar skua and the brown skua, the southern version of the great skua. While they are generally accepted as distinct species it is often hard to separate them in the field, when their distribution overlaps, as in the peninsula, and where they occasionally hybridise.

Any skua with a pale nape and underparts contrasting with darker, uniform upperparts will be a south polar. Like the brown skua. it is a confirmed ship visitor.

Dominic Sherony

South polar skuas (above) and brown skuas both breed in close community with penguins whose eggs and chicks they take.

The Kelp Gull

Abundant and widely scattered through the southern hemisphere, almost to the equator, the kelp gull is the only gull in the Antarctic, southern version of the northern black-backed gulls. They forage the coast and inshore waters. Around scientific stations they scavenge and hope for handouts, remembering the days before new regulations forbade feeding wildlife. They fish for krill but have a particularly close relationship with limpets. *Nacella concinna*, at the extreme south of their range, are in fact the main food, Antarctic beaches and shore slopes are littered with the ravaged shells. The live limpet is superbly adapted to life in a cold climate, enjoying grazing on algae above the waterline in ice-free summers and migrating below the ice in wintertime. It is protected from freezing by a coat of antifreeze mucus. But kelp gulls patrol the tide's edge at low water, swimming and searching for active limpets, taking them by reaching or plunging. The molluscs are swallowed whole, the shells later regurgitated intact, littering the nest area in neat piles.

A kelp gull's midden

Southern Terns

The classic example of 'globe-spanning' is that of the Arctic tern *Sterna paradisiaea*. Most nest in the high Arctic (those breeding around the British Isles are actually at the very southern end of the breeding range) but then migrate from the very top of the world to the Southern Ocean and the continental edge of the Antarctic on the other side of the globe, a journey of some 11,000 miles. In other words they travel an incredible 22,000 miles every year and enjoy a life of perpetual summer.

The Antarctic tern *S. vittata* closely resembles the Arctic tern, but the breeding adult—seen in the austral summer—is naturally in summer plumage, with a black cap and long tail streamers. Unlike the summer visitors it is resident, circumpolar and abundant in the peninsula. A relatively sedentary creature, it even moults on ice-floes or icebergs. It is not a ship-follower.

In the Antarctic season only Antarctic terns are in breeding plumage.

Changing Times, Changing Attitudes

There are many whales to be seen in the Southern Ocean today. Fin, humpback, minke, Southern bottlenose, killer, Commersons dolphin. When I first explored the coastal waters of the Peninsula minke whales were regarded as somewhat diffident creatures which tended to give a wide berth to ships, but minkes have steadily altered their behaviour. These days they seem positively to welcome the chance to approach

Minkes are sociable animals

closely, keeping station or even diving from side to side. Showing great interest in Zodiacs, they chase them, dive under them, spyhop and even breach alongside. Like crabeaters, minke whales feed almost exclusively on krill, and some squid. In turn they are taken by killer whales.

The total world population may have reached the order of half a million, of which perhaps 200,000 are in the Antarctic, where, as pagophilic

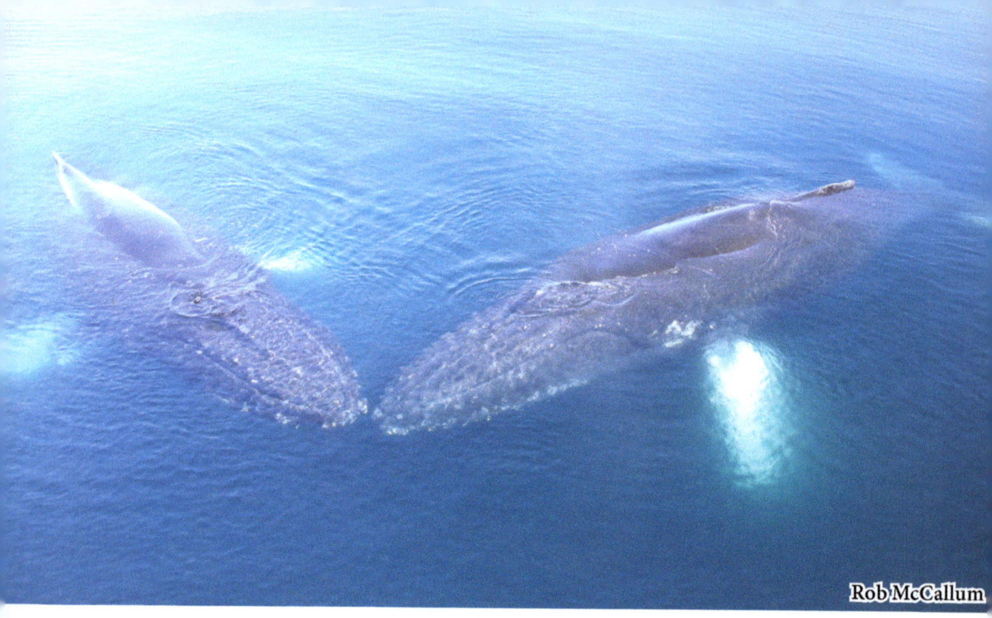
Rob McCallum

(ice-loving) creatures, they are flourishing. In the waters of Neko Harbour they are particularly likely to approach ships or a zodiac full of interest.

Antarctic minkes are hunted under special permits issued by the government of Japan for scientific purposes, allowed by the International Convention for Regulation of Whaling. Consequently, in areas where it is a legal activity, and sometimes where it is not, they are taken by factory-whalers for science and as meat for the domestic Japanese market.

Nineteenth century whaling for minkes

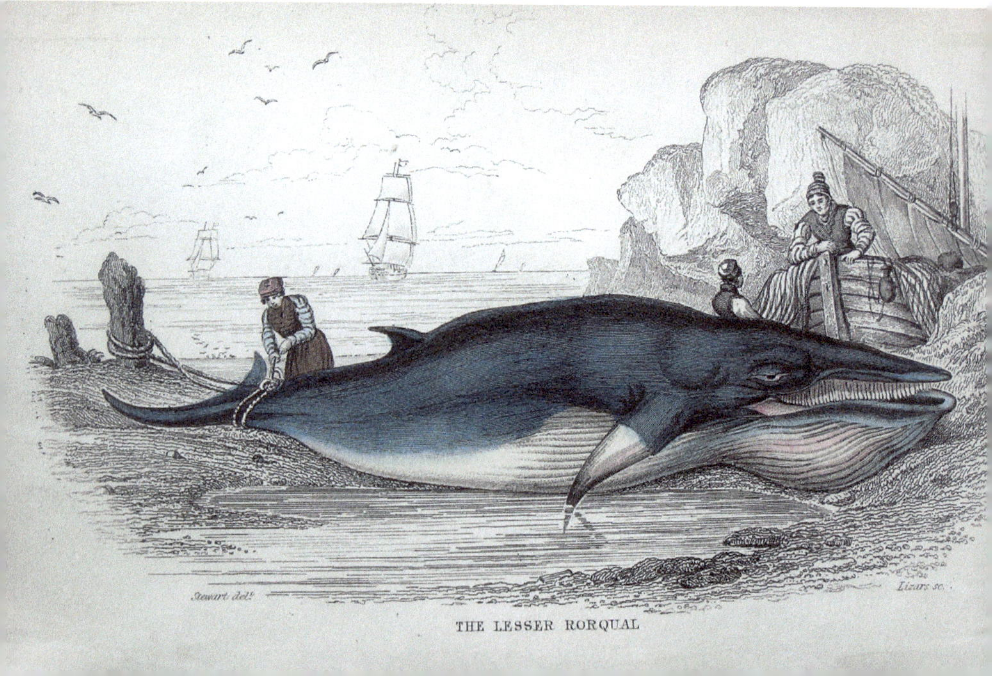
Stewart delt
Lizars sc.
THE LESSER RORQUAL

John Sparks

Humpback whales sometimes show interest and approach a drifting ship. But mostly they are intent on the pursuit of krill, indifferent to spectators. In a feeding session they cruise slowly, at 4–6 knots, with a bushy blow reaching to 3m. They normally blow half a dozen times, and not more than ten, at 15–30 second intervals on surfacing. In diving, their flukes rise high above the surface. Photographs of the flukes are much-prized and have brought immense benefits to our understanding of whale movements. Research is co-ordinated at the College of the Atlantic, Bar Harbour, Maine, where they welcome underside fluke pictures, with date and location, for their Antarctic Humpback Whale Catalog. ahwc@coa.edu

South Georgia

Although South Georgia is a sub-Antarctic island, its position south of the Convergence makes it biologically Antarctic. It is home for prodigious numbers of birds. Thirty breeding and twenty-seven non-breeding species have been recorded. Most are seabirds, of course, but there are two waterfowl. The yellow-billed pintail *Anas georgica* is a large, slender, mottled brown dabbling duck with striking yellow sides to the bill and a prominent pointed tail. It feeds on algae in freshwater ponds in the summer and sheltered bays in the winter.

The speckled teal *A. flavirostris* is a South American species which found its way to South Georgia in the 1960s, only in the area of Cumberland Bay. It is smaller and stockier than the pintail, with a dark head and short tail.

The South Georgia pipit *Anthus antarcticus* is the only passerine bird in the Antarctic, living on insects and spiders in the summer, tideline debris in the winter. Its song somewhat resembles that of the skylark. On off-islands it is fairly common; mainland numbers are certainly improving now that the rats are probably eradicated.

South Georgia pipit

Brian Gratwicke

Albatrosses are well-established on South Georgia. Legendary birds; partly because of their great size but also because they inhabit such remote and storm ridden seas. Early 17th century mariners respected their grace and majesty in flight and generally disapproved of killing them at a time when most birds were valued only for their palatability. They also believed that the souls of drowned sailors were reincarnated in albatrosses, increasing the fear that killing them would bring bad luck. In the late 18th and 19th centuries they were much persecuted for

their meat and their plumage, also taken in significant numbers on hook and line by sailors who made pouches out of their webbed feet, feather rugs from their skins and pipe stems from their long hollow wing bones. Under protection, they recovered, but new threats include drowning in gill-nets, hooking on longlines and choking on plastic waste.

The generic name is the English sailors' corruption of the Portuguese alcatraz for a pelican, a bird which early explorers would have known from the Mediterranean. Albatrosses are divided into two genera, Diomedea and Phoebetria, but in common language the fourteen species are lumped into the 'great albatrosses', the wandering and royal, and the 'small albatrosses', collectively better known to seafarers as mollymawks, from the Dutch mal, foolish, and mok, gull. Another term for them is 'gooney', from the English dialect word for simpleton. These pejorative and richly undeserved epithets were the result partly of seeing albatrosses ashore, out of their element, appearing clumsy, and partly because of their endearing but ill-advised innocence in standing quietly at the nest while being bludgeoned for the pot.

Wandering albatross

Juvenile wandering albatrosses go through the motions of courtship.

Both sexes share an incubation period of 87 days.

Wanderers, the world's largest flying birds, riding the prevailing westerlies of the Southern Ocean.

Vincent Legendre

Light-mantled sooty albatrosses are elegant and handsome sooty-brown birds with a prominently dark head. They nest in solitary fashion or in small loose-knit colonies on islands from South Georgia to the New Zealand sub-Antarctic, returning to the steep slopes, cliff ledges or rocky cliffs, sometimes inland and amongst tussock or ferns, in September or October. Courtship includes the pair flying in close formation with highly synchronised aerobatics, calling with an eerie and wild two-note scream in sensuous abandon.

Milton Sams

No music could be more apt to that romantic desolation. The very spirit of the place! A chord within responds, a chord held silent for a thousand decades while the northern ice-caps slowly died, and man set foot upon the path that may lead up from barbarism. Surprising that a sooty albatross calling to his mate in the cliffs can send such ideas running through the mind.' —Leo Harrison Matthews, South Georgia, c1926.

The King Penguin

Kings are the glory of South Georgia. They breed colonially, choosing raised beaches with easy access to the water and extensive flat or shelving ground. They make no nest but maintain an 'arm's length' territory with vigour. Their breeding arrangements are highly unusual in that the chick may take more than a year to fledge. The consequence is that king penguins cannot breed annually. Although it is possible for them to breed twice in three years, they mostly breed biennially.

The result of the extraordinarily long breeding cycle is that newly hatched chicks and six-month chicks exist side-by-side in a colony occupied continuously by all ages and sizes and plumages. Courting involves raucous antiphonal calling and displays of the brilliant orange patches in head-flagging. Incubating adults work in shifts, displaying the 'Buddha belly' flap of skin that hangs down from the abdomen.

The single egg sits in the warmth of the highly vascular feet, hatching in 54 days. The parents then stand two or three day shifts alternating between incubation and fishing to regurgitate fish soup. At six weeks the chick will weigh over 7kg, reach half the size and weight of adults and moult to thick coats of fluffy chocolate-brown down. This plumage gave them the name 'oakum boys' after their resemblance to the youths who packed the seams of wooden boats with oakum—tarred fibre—to make them watertight.

As they grow, young penguins gather in large numbers to form communal nurseries or crèches as a form of protection against predators. There is no overall 'nanny' in charge, although if danger threatens the chicks may congregate around an adult bird to help ward off attack. Each chick is fed by its own parents, which recognize their offspring both by

In their natural element

calls and by appearance. They face a miserable period while they moult their 'oakum' down and grow their first juvenile feathers before their introduction to the sea and a life of fishing.

On fishing trips king penguins dive to 100 metres but have been recorded at depths greater than 300. Their prey is mainly lanternfish but includes krill. Squid becomes important in the winter. In turn they are the prey of leopard seals and killer whales.

Tim Soper

The only mammals native to South Georgia are the seals and whales, but there have been the inevitable introductions. Both brown rats and house mice were brought to the island by sealers, probably arriving with the earliest explorers in the early 18thcentury. More deliberate and later introductions were cats and rabbits, but these failed to establish wild populations because of the severe winter weather. Perhaps the most surprising encounter for later tourists was with the reindeer *Rangifer tarandus,* first imported in November 1911 by the Norwegian whaling companies to provide both sport and fresh meat. The original three stags and seven hinds, plus later imports, produced descendants which flourished and expanded their range. The numbers were effectively controlled by the availability of tussac, which is rich in carbohydrates. Both rats and deer were the subject of an extermination project, which seems likely to have been a success in 2018.

Liam Quinn

Tussac grass *Poa flabellata* is impressive, it may grow to eleven feet in height and live 300 years. As the long leaves die off, they form a skirt which provides a bed for fur seals and shelter for penguins. Joseph Hooker came to southern waters as assistant surgeon in *Erebus*, with James Clark Ross, in 1842, when he was the first to realise its value as fodder. His father wrote *You are considered the fortunate discoverer of the most wonderful grass that is to make the fortune of all Highland or Irish lairds who have bogs.* Unfortunately, his father was wrong, it didn't do well when introduced into Scotland.

Elephant seals lie scattered among the tussac grass and clumped at one end of the beach, including some enormous bulls. One particularly ponderous bull with glorious tendrils of white mucous dangling from its cavernous nostrils galumphed down the beach, making heavy 'wumph' noises with each successive forward heave of its immense blubbery weight. One could almost feel the earth shake as it rumbled by. It made its way towards its chums which were all busily engaged in an intense bout of sleep. Sleeping in elephant seals isn't complete without the customary expulsion of gas from all orifices, and this group seemed particularly productive. It was quite a hot day, and since elephant seals are so very blubberous they were getting a bit warm, lying there cooking in the sun (a few even had steam rising off their backs.) They help ward off the sun's rays by flinging sand over their backs using their short fore-flippers. So in addition to the belching, farting and grunting there were intermittent sprays of sand into the air.

Southern elephants are the largest seals in the world today. Reversing the norm though, the bull is substantially larger than the cow. The name comes partly from the elephantine size but also from the extraordinary trunk-like proboscis of the bull, which is inflatable, and attains its full splendour when the animal is in its eighth year. Their food consists mainly of squid, caught in deep diving. Dives last in excess of thirty minutes and have been recorded to 1,000m. Cheek teeth are reduced to widely-spaced pegs, an adaptation associated with the squid diet. At sea, they gorge themselves and fatten so that their blubber reserves sustain them during the long breeding and moulting period ashore, during which they fast. Pregnant cows come ashore on traditional beaches in September/October, hauling out a few days before the pup is born, in mid-October. The bulls are already on the beaches, establishing dominance amongst themselves and guarding a harem of several dozen cows. In establishing their territory they produce a bubbling roar of impressive loudness, aided by the resonating chamber of the proboscis. Most of the rumbustious behaviour is over by early December and the beaches become relatively quiet. On dispersal they go to sea, and travel widely, returning to the shore in late summer to gather at muddy and stinking wallows for the 40 days of moult. This is a time when their gregarious nature shows, for they lie closely side by side in close companionship—behaviour known as thigmotaxis.

A nice example of thigmotaxis, in which animals enjoy the stimulus of physical contact.

Strategic withdrawal. Avoiding the stimulus of close contact.

Richard Stennes

Happy he who like Ulysses has made a great journey.
—Joachim du Bellay (1522-1560)

Andrew Shiva

Acknowledgments

Many shipmates shared the pleasures and challenges of the Southern Ocean and I warmly remember all of them for their support, in particular Gilles Allard, Sisse Brimberg & Cotton Coulson, Jennifer & Peter Clement, Kim Crosbie, Chris Edwards, Amanda Ellerbeck, Martin Enckell, Fabrice Genevois, Brandon Harvey, Bob Headland, Barbara Jones, Stefan Kindberg, Judy & Norm Lasca, Lars-Eric & Ruriko Lindblad, Roger Lovegrove, Colin McNulty, Mike Messick, Rinie van Meurs, Mike Murphy, Pete Oxford, Katarina Salén, Monica Schillat, Darrel Schoeling, Jonathan Shackleton, John Sparks, Anna Sutcliffe, Pat Toomey, Ingrid Visser, Kara Weller, Allan White, Richard White, Erica & Lars Wikander.

I want to celebrate the masters of the splendid ships I have had the privilege of joining down south: Pavel Ankudinov, Petr Golikov, Filipp Kolesnikov, Sergey Kostusev, Karl-Ulrich Lampe, Andrey Rudenko, Leif Skog, Viktor Vasilyev, Alexey Zakalashnyuk; and the ships, themselves: *Alla Tarasova, Artemis, Akademik Ioffe, Crystal Symphony, Grigoriy Mikheev, Kapitan Khlebnikov, Polar Star, Professor Khromov, Professor Molchanov, Professor Multanovskiy, Lindblad Explorer, Lyubov Orlova, National Geographic Explorer, Rotterdam, Sea Spirit.*

Author

Tony Soper is a writer and broadcaster. In a first career in radio and television with the BBC's Natural History Unit he travelled in search of wilderness islands and their wildlife. As expedition leader and lecturer he circumnavigated the Antarctic in icebreakers, exploring from Kerguelen to Macquarie in research vessels. His published works concentrate on marine wildlife, islands and the seashore with guides to high latitudes which are stowed in the intrepid polar traveller's backpack.

Index

Albatross, 101
, Black-browed 65
, Lt-mantled Sooty 15, 104
, Wandering 11, 103
Amundsen, Roald 38, 47
Andersson, Johan 42, 43
Antarctic, first sighting 16
Antarctic, 42
Archipelago, Palmer 44
Astrolabe 26
Audubon, John James 83
Auk, family 82
, Great 82, 83
Aurora 49

Banks, Grand 82-83
Bay, Hope 42
, Whaler's 60, 61
Belgica 38, 39
Bellingshausen, Fabian 16
Bellows, Neptunes 19
Belt, Banana 19
Betsey, 18
Bogeymen 92
Borchgrevink, Carsten 40
Bransfield, Edward 16
Buenos Aires 44
Bumstead, Blondie 88
, Dagwood 88

Campbell, David 7
Cannon, harpoon 30, 31
Cape Denison 53
, Good Hope 80
, Horn 63
, Royds 51
, Wellmet 43
Center, US National Ice 73
Chanticleer, HMS 20
Charcot, Jean-Baptiste 44
Cherry-Garrard, Apsley 47, 54
Chicken, Mother Carey's 70
Clusius, Carolus 81
Convergence, Antarctic 9, 99
Cook, Captain James 12-17
Cook, Frederick 38
Cove, Pendulum 60

d'Urville, Dumont 26
Diaz, Bartolomeo 80
Discovery, RRS 47
Doodle, Yankee 88
Drake, Sir Francis 10, 11
Drift, West wind 62

Erebus, HMS 27
Eruption, volcanic 60
Expedition, Australasian Antarctic 53
, Belgian Antarctic 38

, British Antarctic 40
, British Graham Land 58
, Discovery 47
, Imperial Trans-Antarctic 54
, Nimrod 50
, Swedish South Polar 42
, Terra Nova 47
Exploitation 17

Fanning, Captain Edmund 18
Foster, Captain Henry 20
Foyne, Sven 31
Français 44
Frithiof 44
Fuego, Tierra del 63

Garfowl 81
Georgia, South, Biologically 100
, Discovery 14
, Introductions 108
, Native mammals 108
, Reindeer 108
, Sealing 17
, Whaling stations 31
Gerlache, Adrien de 38
Grass, Tussac 109
Greene, Captain Daniel 18
Grytviken 31
, Church 32
Gull, Kelp 94
Gylden, Hans 44

Harbord, Arthur 50
Hatch, Joseph 36
Havilland, de 58, 59
Head, Bailie 89
Hektor, company 31
Hero 19
Hodges, William 13
Hofman, Justin 2

Ice 74-75
Iceberg, Tabular 73
Irizar, Julian 44
Island, Deception, 31, 58, 59, 60
, Funk 83
, Goudier 85
, King George 6
, Macquarie 36
, Paulet 43, 44
, Possession 27
, Seymour 42
, Snow Hill 42, 44, 45

Jane, Brig 20
Jesus-bird 70

Kerguelen 20
Khlebnikov, Kapitan 6, 75

117

Index, continued

Land, Adélie 26
  , Dronning Maud 16
  , Graham 44, 58
  , South Victoria 40
Larsen, Carl 31, 42
Lazarev, Captain 16
Lights, Southern 49
Lockroy, Port 85

Magellan, Ferdinand 81
Matthews, Leo Harrison 104
Mawson, Douglas 53
Mirnyi 16
Molchanov, Professor 62
Moth, Fox 58
Murdoch, W G Burn 20

Nancy 18
Nordenskjold, Otto 42, 44

O'Brien, Conor Cruise 80
Oakum 107
Ocean, Southern 16, 17
Otter, de Havilland 59

Palmer, Nathaniel 19
Passage, Drake 11, 62, 64
Penguin, Adélie 27, 40, 41
  , Chinstrap 89-91
  , Emperor 6, 28, 76-78
  , Gentoo 84
  , King 37, 105-107
  , Macaroni 86, 87
Penguins, Nomenclature 81-82
  , Classification 80
  , Northern hemisphere 92
Petrel, Antarctic 66
  , Cape 66
  , derivation 70
  , Giant 34, 35
  , Snow 72
Petrel, steam catcher 30
Piloto Pardo, steam tug 60
Pingüim 84
Pinguis 82
Pintail, Yellow-billed 99
Pipit, South Georgia 99
Plateau, Antarctic 47
Plunge, Polar 61
Pole, South 47
Port Foster 20, 31
Prion, Antarctic 68
  , Fairy 68

Quest 57

Razorbill, Giant 81, 82
Resolution, HMS 13
Ross, James Clark 27-29
Røst 92

Rothera 59
Rymill, John Riddoch 58

Scott, Robert Falcon 47-49
Seal, Crabeater 24
  , Elephant 5, 20, 29, 110, 111
  , Leopard 22, 23
  , Ross 25
  , Southern fur 17
  , Weddell 22
Shackleton, Ernest 51-57
Shearwater, Sooty 62
Sheathbill, Snowy 67, 79
Shelf, Ross Ice 48
Shetlands, South 16, 42, 58
Ships, Factory 31
Shuckburgh, Richard 88
Skua, Brown 67, 93, 94
  , South Polar, 93, 94
Smith, Captain William 16
Soapine 31
Sonnerat, Pierre 89
Southern Cross, steamship 40
Stinker 34, 69-70
Survey, British Antarctic 59
  , Falkland Islands Dependencies 59

Tabarin, Operation 59
Teal, Speckled 99
Tennyson, Lord 4
Tern, Antarctic 95
  , Arctic 9, 95
Terra Australis 16
Terror, HMS 27
Tour, Italian Grand 87
Trust, NZ Antarctic 41, 51-52
  , UK Antarctic Heritage 85

Uruguay Corvette 44, 46
Ushuaia 62

Vostok, sloop 16

War, American Revolutionary 88
Weddell, James 21, 22
Whale, Blue 31
  , Fin 71
  , Humpback 99
  , Minke 97-98
Whaling, International Convention 98
Whisky, Mackinlay's 52
Williams, brig 16
Wilson, Alexander 70
  , Edward 70
Wind, katabatic 53
Wonders, Day of 44
Worm, Ole 81

Zélée 26

Guides by Tony Soper

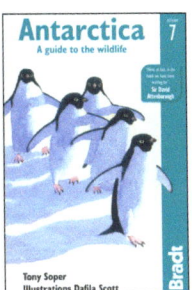

Antarctica, a guide to the wildlife
Bradt 2018 (7th edn)

Few people can claim to be thoroughly familiar with Antarctic wildlife. Most of us visiting the deep south are doing so for the first time and thirst for some authoritative guidance. Here…is the book we have been waiting for. —Sir David Attenborough

For anyone Antarctica-bound, this is the book. —Keith Shackleton

The Arctic, a guide to coastal wildlife
Bradt 2019 (4th edn)

The best wildlife coverage of any of the guide books.—BBC Wildlife

Beautifully written, engaging text. —WWF Wildlife bulletin

The Northwest Passage
Venture Books 2019

The indispensable guide—attractive package which brings a fascinating place alive. —Amazon

The Northeast Passage
Venture Books 2020

Thorough and enjoyable, the first and only guidebook to the history and wildlife of Russia's arctic coast. —Nina Maclean

www.ingramcontent.com/pod-product-compliance
Lightning Source LLC
Chambersburg PA
CBHW042050290426
44110CB00001B/11